# HAUNTED CEMETERIES

## AROUND THE WORLD

BY ALICIA Z. KLEPEIS

CAPSTONE PRESS

a capstone imprint

Snap Books are published by
Capstone, 1710 Roe Crest Drive,
North Mankato, Minnesota 56003.
www.mycapstone.com

For information regarding permission, write to Capstone, 1710 Roe Crest Drive, North Mankato, Minnesota 56003.

Library of Congress Cataloging-in-Publication Data
Names: Klepeis, Alicia, 1971- author.
Title: Haunted cemeteries around the world / by Alicia Z. Klepeis.
Description: North Mankato, Minnesota : Capstone Press, [2017] | Series: Snap books. It's haunted! | Includes bibliographical references and index.
Identifiers: LCCN 2016034860| ISBN 9781515738619 (library binding) | ISBN 9781515738695 (ebook (pdf)
Subjects: LCSH: Haunted cemeteries--Juvenile literature. | Haunted places--Juvenile literature. | Ghosts--Juvenile literature.
Classification: LCC BF1474.3 .K59 2017 | DDC 133.1/22--dc23
LC record available at https://lccn.loc.gov/2016034860

**Editorial Credits**

Mari Bolte, editor; Kristi Carlson, designer; Wanda Winch, media researcher; Gene Bentdahl, production specialist

**Photo Credits**

Alamy: Andria Patino, 27, Images-USA, 26, RM USA, 28, Stockimo/Robert Christopher, 16; Bridgeman Images: © Historic England/John Gay (manipulated photo), 21, Ken Welsh/Private Collection/English School, 11, Travelshots/© Peter Phipp, 18; Dreamstime: Catalinapanait, 10, Dirkwenzel, 22, 24, 25, Mail50777, 14; Joe Gilhooley Photography, 13; Newscom: Zuma Press/Graham Whitby Boot – Allstar, 6; Painting by Dimitri Fouquet, 29; Reuters: Haider Ala, 5; Shutterstock: Alistair Hobbs, 9, A-R-T, calligraphic design, Don Cline, 19, Eisfrei, flower leaf design, Fantom666, grunge background, Heartland Arts, 12, HiSunnySky, floral background, ilolab, brick wall design, iolya, statue shadow, jakkapan, retro frame design, Jane Rix, cover (bottom), janniwet, antique frame, kzww, wood wall, Leremy, ornate sign design, LilGraphie, photo corners design, LovArt, globe design, Nature Art, pink rose design, Neil Lang, cover (top), PeterPhoto123, oval frame, rayjunk, vintage frame, spaxiax, stone wall background

Printed in China.
092016    007892

# TABLE OF CONTENTS

# WHAT REMAINS BEHIND

As nightfall approaches, you wander along the twisting, turning pathways of a cemetery. Light fog drifts overhead, making it hard to see very far. It sounds as if a heavy old gate is creaking in the distance. Is someone else here?

Feeling spooked, you cautiously make your way through the cemetery. Moss-covered gravestones mark the lives of people who have passed on. Giant **mausoleums** cast shadows on the ground. Do ghosts lurk inside these tombs? Or do they wander freely? Perhaps these spirits are following close on the heels of those visiting departed loved ones. A high-pitched squeal sounds nearby. It might be a mouse. Or it could be a ghost. Is it a friendly ghost? Or is it the ghost of a long-dead criminal?

Even if you don't believe in ghosts, cemeteries can be creepy places for anyone. No one can say for sure whether ghosts exist. But one thing is certain—many cemeteries around the world are frightful places that inspire terror in those who visit.

Wadi Al-Salaam Cemetery in Najaf, Iraq

### FACT

The Wadi Al-Salaam Cemetery in Iraq is the world's largest place of burial. Over the past 1,400 years, millions of Muslims have been laid to rest there—and this tradition continues today. Wadi Al-Salaam is the only active cemetery in the world with this much history.

**mausoleum:** a large building that holds tombs

# FOREST LAWN MEMORIAL GARDENS
## FORT LAUDERDALE, FLORIDA, USA

**Ghosts from recent burials have reportedly been seen wandering freely about the cemetery grounds.**

## BOXERS AND BALL GOWNS

Spiky shadows cloak visitors to Forest Lawn Memorial Gardens. Among the graves stands the tall mausoleum of boxer Rocky Marciano and his wife Barbara. Visitors have claimed to take photographs of ghosts resembling Rocky and Barbara. Some people say that the pair likes to linger near their gravesite. But their ghosts are not the only spirits said to roam Forest Lawn.

A **specter** known as Diane wears lots of makeup and a long pink gown. She appears out of nowhere, walking in front of cars and spooking unsuspecting drivers. Diane always manages to disappear just before making contact.

Even if you don't see a ghost at Forest Lawn Memorial Gardens, you may hear one. This is not a silent cemetery. Ghost hunters have **EVP** recordings of voices saying, *"leave me alone!"* and, *"Please come back."* Who knows which ghost will make itself known next?

Rocky, Barbara, and Diane are three of the most active spirits lurking around Forest Lawn Memorial Gardens. However, there are said to be many others.

One commonly seen spirit is the ghost of a young hippie with long, light-colored hair. He wears bell-bottom pants and a tie-dyed shirt. He has been seen sitting by himself all over the cemetery. Visitors have started calling this ghost Grover.

According to legend, Grover regularly attends funerals. Unafraid of the living, he walks right up to mourning visitors and asks them if they have a light. When they turn to answer, he vanishes.

---

**specter:** a ghost

**EVP:** sounds or voices heard during electronic recordings that can't be explained; EVP stands for electronic voice phenomenon

# MOUNT PLEASANT CEMETERY
## SINGAPORE

### BLACK MAGIC AND VAMPIRES

Drooping Angsana trees and lush jungle surround Singapore's Mount Pleasant Cemetery. Tombs line both sides of the path that snakes through this haunted graveyard. Some are cracked and falling apart. At night it's almost impossible to see peoples' final resting places.

In medieval times, Javanese people lived on this land. Village **shamans** known as *bomohs* are said to have practiced black magic. During these early days, the *bomohs* tried to create and control vampires known as pontianaks. The pontianaks were forced to work as servants or even **assassins**. Eventually the village vanished and the land became a cemetery.

Many people believe pontianaks still haunt the land, flying over the cemetery's trees by night. According to one horrific story, men who died on the open ground here had their bodies shredded by pontianaks. Their guts were scattered across the cemetery. Tales say pontianaks use their razor-sharp fingernails to tear into their victim's stomachs to get to their organs. Visitors believe they can hear the pontianaks' spine-chilling laughs echo through the graveyard.

Pontianak-like vampires exist in legends throughout southeast Asia, especially in Malaysia and Indonesia.

## PONTIANAKS

It is believed that a pontianak is a spirit created when a woman who died in childbirth becomes **undead**. These spirits are beautiful but deadly, seeking revenge and terrorizing villages.

Many people believe that they can fend off a pontianak's attack by having a sharp object, such as a nail, with them. Plunging the nail into the back of the vampire's neck is the only way to defeat her.

**shaman:** a tribal religious leader and healer

**assassin:** a person who kills an important person, such as a president.

**undead:** technically dead but still animate; zombies are a form of the undead

# GREYFRIARS KIRKYARD
## EDINBURGH, SCOTLAND

A kirk (church) has stood on the kirkyard grounds since 1620. The kirk today was built in the early 17th century.

## STOLEN BODIES IN THE KIRKYARD

Ghoulish figures and eerie angels of death greet visitors at Greyfriars Kirkyard. But creepy tombstones are the last thing to worry about here.

Metal grates cover some of the graves. Why? Greyfriars Kirkyard has a long history of dealing with body snatchers.

In the early 1800s, thieves stole **cadavers** from Greyfriars for use at the University of Edinburgh's medical school. To keep bodies safe, heavy iron cages called mortsafes were placed over graves. Long iron rods held the mortsafes in place. Once the bodies were decomposed enough to be unappealing to grave robbers, the mortsafes were removed and used for the next deceased person.

Disturbing the dead can come with great consequences. Many believe that Greyfriars Kirkyard is home to the MacKenzie **poltergeist**. Stories say that George MacKenzie's spirit was released when a homeless man seeking a place to rest broke into MacKenzie's mausoleum.

**FACT**

The MacKenzie poltergeist is known to be aggressive, harming late-night visitors. In life MacKenzie was responsible for punishing, imprisoning, and torturing thousands of people known as Covenanters because of their religious beliefs. People called their torturer Bluidy (Bloody) MacKenzie.

**cadaver:** a dead body that is used for medical or scientific purposes

**poltergeist:** a ghost that causes physical events, such as objects moving

**Greyfriars Kirkyard was first used as a burial ground in 1562.**

Those who visit Greyfriars Kirkyard do so at their own risk. People taking nighttime tours of the kirkyard have experienced strange smells, numbness, and mysterious injuries. According to a Scottish newspaper, this haunted cemetery has been the site of 450 documented attacks on visitors. Another 140 people have collapsed while visiting.

Tour guide David Polluck said, "In the two and a half years I have done this job, I have carried out 19 people unconscious. I have even felt myself being punched hard and yet there was nothing there in front of me." Could Bluidy MacKenzie be there, carrying out his life's work ... in death?

## AN UNFINISHED EXORCISM

In 2000 a man named Colin Grant attempted to perform an **exorcism**. He hoped to drive the evil spirits from the kirkyard. While in the middle of the ceremony, he told people he felt the presence of evil forces. Fearing for his life, Grant quickly left.

Grant died of a sudden heart attack two months after attempting the exorcism. Even today, many people believe the MacKenzie poltergeist punishes anyone who disturbs his final resting place.

Tourists and thrill-seekers can visit the kirkyard at night for paranormal tours.

exorcism: a ceremony done to get rid of a spirit

# SAN MICHELE
## VENICE, ITALY

Very few of the dead are permanently buried on San Michele.
After about ten years, they are dug up and cremated,
or moved to the mainland.

## ISLAND OF THE DEAD

Venice, Italy is built on a series of islands. There isn't much land space. But people have lived there since the 5th century. The lack of land created a problem—where to put the dead? For many centuries, Venetians buried people within churches or even below the city's paving stones.

When Napoleon conquered the city in 1797, his inspectors surveyed the area and declared that burying people inside the city was unsanitary. Since that time, the dead have been buried on an island called San Michele.

The inhabitants of San Michele aren't trapped there, though. On the night before All Souls' Day, which takes place on November 2, the dead are said to leave the island. They travel across the lagoon and into Venice, strolling through the streets. When a ghost reaches the front door of his or her former home, he or she sits by the kitchen fire until the day is over.

All Souls' Day is a time to remember the dead. A special ferry takes people to San Michele to visit loved ones' graves on this special day. Pictures, memorials, gifts, and flowers decorate the cemetery. However, it is considered unlucky to actually see the dead as they return to their homes. In some areas of Italy it is common for the whole family to leave the house when the dead are expected.

## HOLIDAYS THAT CELEBRATE THE DEAD

Dia de los Muertos—the Day of the Dead—lasts three days and overlaps with All Saints' Day. During both holidays, people remember those who have passed on. But while All Saints' Day honors the dead, Dia de los Muertos welcomes their return. Some people believe that the souls of those who have died return to earth to visit with family and friends. The day celebrates those who have died; the food, drinks, and activities they loved in life are enjoyed, and offerings are left in case they care to return.

# HIGHGATE CEMETERY
## LONDON, ENGLAND

**Highgate Cemetery stretches over 17 acres (8 hectares) of land.**

## THERE'S ALWAYS ROOM FOR ONE MORE ...

Human bodies need to be buried quickly. But what happens when there's nowhere to put them? Back in the 1800s, the population of London, England, skyrocketed, making it the largest city in the world. But with more living people comes more dead. The churchyards where people were typically buried quickly became overcrowded.

One 1843 study estimated that around 40 people died each day—and they all needed to be buried. Bodies and coffins were stacked on top of each other. Sometimes bodies were dug up at night to be burned in mass **pyres** to make room for the newly deceased. A substance called quicklime was thrown on bodies to help them decompose faster. Bodies were left anywhere there was space, including backyards and alleyways. Exhumed bodies were dumped, and the now-empty coffins were sold to the poor as firewood.

In the early- and mid-1800s, seven private cemeteries were established outside of London. Highgate was one of those cemeteries. A hilly location and carefully-thought-out architecture and landscaping made Highgate Cemetery an appealing place for the wealthy to be buried.

**FACT**

There are more than 170,000 people buried in 53,000 graves in Highgate Cemetery. Famous graves include Douglas Adams, George Eliot, and Patrick Caulfield.

**pyre:** a pile of wood built to burn a dead body for a funeral

Large vaults were built at the center of the cemetery.
These areas are known as Egyptian Avenue and
the Circle of Lebanon.

By the start of the 1900s, tens of thousands of people rested forever at Highgate. By then, Highgate was well known as a haunted place. Frightened visitors shared tales of their ghostly encounters in the local newspapers. The cemetery lost much of its financial support as the most desirable spots were filled. Large tombs went unmaintained as family members moved away or died out. Slowly the cemetery declined from a fancy place of burial for the rich to a crumbling ruin. Some said that cults were using the cemetery for strange and scary ceremonies.

In the early 1970s tales of a vampire in Highgate began to spread across the countryside. People described a tall, dark man who floated above the graves. One man claimed the vampire hypnotized him and drained him of so much energy that he fainted. Some believe the vampire was summoned by one of the cults that met at the cemetery.

Hundreds of supernatural hunters participated in a search for the Highgate Vampire. Nothing unusual was found that day; however, years later one of the hunters claimed to have destroyed the vampire forever.

Since 1975 a restoration group has worked to preserve the cemetery's monuments and clear the overgrown landscape.

## SPIRITS AND SHADOWS

No one is certain whether the Highgate Vampire still hides amidst the shadows. But people continue to see supernatural events and otherworldly beings here.

Some visitors have heard about a tall man dressed in black who walks through walls. A young mother claimed to see a ghost on a bicycle. A late 19th century nurse has been seen in the background of modern photographs.

One man claimed to see the glowing red eyes of a hideous ghostlike creature through the cemetery's rusting iron gates. Another visitor was assaulted by a frightening creature while walking around the grounds. It seemed to pop out from the cemetery wall. The man was saved when an approaching car's headlights made the spirit disappear into thin air.

The ghost of an elderly woman with long gray hair is a common sight at the cemetery. Believers say she searches for her children whom she is claimed to have murdered.

Were these **apparitions** really there? No one can say for sure.

---

**apparition:** the visible appearance of a ghost

---

More than one visitor to Highgate Cemetery has
left after running into supernatural beings.

# PARIS CATACOMBS
## PARIS, FRANCE

**Some signs in the catacombs explain where the bones came from. Others hold spooky or ominous quotes.**

## EMPIRE OF THE DEAD

More than 2 million people live, breathe, and thrive in the city of Paris, France. But just below the city's streets is a completely different metropolis—the **catacombs** of the dead.

Paris has been inhabited for thousands of years. It was named the capital of France in AD 508. By the 1200s Paris was the most populated city in the western world. By the 1600s the number of people who had lived and died in Paris was staggering.

The city's cemeteries were overcrowded, with nowhere to lay the dead to rest. Bodies lay stacked on top of each other. The smell of death wafted through the air. In 1780 torrential rains caused a wall around the city's largest cemetery to collapse. Corpses floated into neighboring areas, damaging soil and water and spreading disease. It was clear something needed to be done.

Alexandre Lenoir, a police officer, came up with a clever, but creepy solution. More than 180 miles (290 kilometers) of tunnels existed below Paris. The tunnels were former limestone quarries created when stone was removed to build the city. Lenoir thought the cemeteries could be emptied into the tunnels.

Starting in 1786, workers dug up bodies from cemeteries across Paris. Bones were added into the underground tunnels until about 1859. In the end, the remains of between 6 and 7 million people were reburied there.

At first, bones were piled high in random heaps. In 1810 the inspector of the quarries had the bones organized into the more visually-pleasing displays the catacombs are known for.

**FACT**

People who enter the catacombs illegally are called cataphiles.

catacomb: an underground cemetery

**Some of the oldest bones in the catacombs are more than 1,200 years old.**

It's no surprise that spirits may lurk here. Ghostly figures have been reported in the catacombs' passageways. Some visitors claim to have seen cloudy, unidentifiable shapes in their photos. Others say that they have captured strange lights or orbs on film.

Hundreds of thousands of visitors tour the catacombs every year. It's not unusual for visitors to the catacombs to want to leave mid-tour. Ghostly touches, ranging from brief to violent, have been reported. Others get the feeling they are being watched or followed. Strange footsteps, shadows, and sounds make the experience even more creepy. A few people have even reported that they feel sad or drained of energy while in the catacombs.

It is said that many who have entered the catacombs without a guide have never returned. Between miles of twisting tunnels, dark corners, and piles of bones, it's no surprise that it's easy to get lost or frightened.

Ghost hunters have made EVP recordings inside the Paris catacombs. Sometimes they are just strange clicks. But other times they resemble screams. What could be making these sounds? Perhaps the secret is best left with those trapped in the tomb beneath Paris.

Tourists are only allowed access to 1.2 miles (2 kilometers) of the approximately 124 miles (200 km) that make up the catacombs.

## FACT

Subterranean cemeteries exist in other locations around the world. Peru, Italy, Egypt, Malta, Austria, and the Czech Republic all have catacombs.

**The St. Louis Cemetery is just outside New Orleans' historic French Quarter.**

## TOMB OF THE VOODOO QUEEN

New Orleans was built on swampy land. Because holes in the ground quickly fill with water, people who die there must be buried aboveground. Over many years tombs, elaborate mausoleums, and crypts decorated with sculptures and artwork were built. These structures, grouped together, began to resemble small settlements. People started calling them the Cities of the Dead.

St. Louis Cemetery No. 1 is New Orleans' oldest City of the Dead. Its maze of tombs is the final resting place for more than 100,000 souls. Its most famous resident is Marie Laveau, also known as the **Voodoo** Queen of New Orleans. Many people visit her white tomb each year. Some visit out of respect, or because they are fascinated with Marie. Others come because they wish to ask the Voodoo Queen a favor.

The cemetery dates back to 1789.

**Voodoo:** a religion that began in Africa; Voodoo is also spelled Vodou

In 2014 the organization Save Our Cemeteries spent $10,000 to restore Marie's tomb.

## WAKING THE QUEEN

Legend says that to wake Marie, seekers must draw an X on her tomb, turn around three times, knock on the tomb, and say their wish. If their wish comes true, they must return to the tomb and draw a circle around the X. An offering for Marie should be left too. Common offerings include coins, candles, flowers, and beads.

Marie doesn't sit by, quietly answering wishes. Her ghost is said to haunt the cemetery too. She has been seen wandering between the tombs, mumbling curses under her breath. Some say she can take the form of a cat with glowing red eyes. The cat can walk through Marie's sealed tomb door, vanishing inside. Marie also had a **familiar** in life—a large black snake known as Zombi. Many believe Zombi haunts the cemetery with his mistress.

**FACT**

Marie Laveau's gravesite is the second-most visited gravesite in the United States, after Elvis Presley's place of burial, Graceland, in Memphis, Tennessee.

In 2013 someone snuck into the cemetery and painted Marie's tomb pink. To prevent further **vandalization**, everyone who tours the cemetery now must enter with a licensed tour guide.

---

**familiar:** a demon that obeys a witch; familiars are often said to take the form of an animal

**vandalize:** to needlessly damage property

# GLOSSARY

**apparition** (ap-uh-RISH-uhn)—the visible appearance of a ghost

**assassin** (uh-SA-suhn)—a person who kills an important person, such as a president

**cadaver** (kuh-DA-vuhr)—a dead body that is used for medical or scientific purposes

**catacomb** (CAT-uh-kohm)—an underground cemetery

**cremate** (KREE-mate)—to burn a dead body to ashes

**exorcism** (EK-sohr-siz-uhm)—a ceremony done to get rid of a spirit

**familiar** (fuh-MIL-yuhr)—a demon that obeys a witch; familiars are often said to take the form of an animal

**mausoleum** (maw-suh-LEE-uhm)—a large building that holds tombs

**poltergeist** (POLL-ter-guyst)—a ghost that causes physical events, such as objects moving

**pyre** (PYER)—a pile of wood built to burn a dead body for a funeral

**shaman** (SHAY-muhn)—a tribal religious leader and healer

**specter** (SPEK-tur)—a ghost

**undead** (uhn-DED)—technically dead but still animate; zombies are a form of the undead

**vandalize** (VAN-duhl-ize)—to needlessly damage property

**Voodoo** (VOO-doo)—a religion that began in Africa; Voodoo is also spelled Vodou

# READ MORE

**Chandler, Matt**. *Bachelor's Grove Cemetery And Other Haunted Places Of The Midwest*. North Mankato, Minn: Capstone Press, 2014.

**Owings, Lisa.** *Ghosts in Cemeteries*. Minneapolis: Bellwether Media, Inc., 2017.

**Summers, Alex**. *Haunted Battlefields and Cemeteries*. Vero Beach, Fla.: Rourke Educational Media, 2016.

# INTERNET SITES

FactHound offers a safe, fun way to find Internet sites related to this book. All of the sites on FactHound have been researched by our staff.

Here's all you do:
Visit *www.facthound.com*
Type in this code: 9781515738619

 Check out projects, games and lots more at
**www.capstonekids.com**

# INDEX

# READ ALL THE IT'S HAUNTED TITLES!
## Titles in This Set